T0381341

Mother Goose Goes Broadway

Antonia Gazetas Weese

{Script for Stage Production}

Or

A Beautiful Educational Story

Mother Goose Goes Broadway
Written and Produced by
Antonia Gazetas Weese

AuthorHouse™
1663 Liberty Drive
Bloomington, IN 47403
www.authorhouse.com
Phone: 1-800-839-8640

First published by AuthorHouse 09/12/2011

ISBN: 978-1-4634-4180-7 (sc)

Library of Congress Control Number: 2011914025

Printed in the United States of America

authorHOUSE®

Acknowledgement

I want to thank God, my mother Zambelia my father George in spirit. My husband Tim my daughter Desiree and my friend Jeff, and Frankie Sam, they are the reasons I was able to finish my book, and put on the educational musical production staged for the first time in the Smokey Mountains of Tennessee.

All the parents who helped me effortlessly and of course the students the precious students. The young adults and students who were part of this production thank you I learned a lot. All the paid professionals thank you, you all worked very hard. God bless you all my life co-exists with God, Jesus Christ, Family, Friends and music. I want to thank my little granddaughter Alexis who performed in this current show the book has a lot to do with her life. I love you Alexis you handled yourself well. My daughter Desiree well what can I say but I love you with all my might thank you and thanks to you and Doc for your donations. George my oldest grandson thank you for inspiring me to go on when I wanted to throw in the towel I love you. Toni you dear, encouraged me as well as gave me a run for my money so to speak I love you. Mylea you gave me a struggle but thank you for all the back up vocals I love you and Niki your pushing me and also your encouragement and like Toni you both are beautiful but just keep your heads on straight your both very good and I love you Niki. Last Vassilia wish you were there I love you more than you know as a loving sister. Stephen, my little grandson, I know you could not be there to perform but I love you very much.

and all the special people I won't mention your name I respect your privacy but know I love you all very very much without you don't know what I would have done. My confidant, my new found friend, love you guys.

and finally I have to remember all my precious friends who passed away while this all was going on you are remembered and loved by the Gazetas family.

Antonia

4

Story Line

Mother Goose Goes Broadway is about a young woman and a young man wanting success and stardom. They are achieving their hopes and dreams, while doing what is right. The world is different today compared to twenty years ago. We are going into galaxies of unknown regions, and we need to keep love in the air and unite as one, or we will lose sight of our youths.

With all the overdevelopment of homes and buildings destroying our precious resources, we need to replenish the trees and plants, and people need to stop littering and polluting the water. The musical is just that—ways to bring love, hope, and unity and a reminder to plant trees, watch our water, and conserve our resources. This will give help to our communities. Working through the arts is one way to reach our kids. Teachers & parents need motivation and support.

What you are about to read will take you back to a time when the way of life was simple. For those who are able to watch it performed live, enjoy. *Students perform Mother Goose Goes Broadway, the story,* in this book serves as the script. Those who can catch a performance will notice that the colors and sounds of the production are beautiful. Moreover, enjoy watching the people smile and the cast pushing themselves, and some performing for the first time. For those who are reading the book, this will help you learn to enjoy reading and hopefully help you to reminisce of the good times in your life. The author wants to help the people.

The story opens with Jill in her hometown. Finally having graduated from high school where in reality she passed her GED at the adult high school, she arrives home and goes to her bedroom. She begins to read the local newspaper to find that she has a second chance at stardom. She feels it is a new beginning in her life. She sees that Mother Goose is in town. However, what is in store for Jill will amaze her. Quickly, she locates her friend Jack and finds out that he never left the town, much to her surprise. Jill arranges to meet him at the community theater stage door to see if they can talk to Mother Goose.

Jill is feeling awareness and hope at the thought of being able to be a part of theater, which Jack and Jill both wanted for so long.

Allow your mind to release and enjoy. Leave your worries at bay for today. In addition, visit Mother Goose and her storybook character friends while they take you to a musical place of love, music, and lots of color and joy.

As a storyteller, Antonia (the author) chose Mother Goose to spread cheer and unity as a way to educate youths of all ages, to look out for the curves in life. Education is the key to health, wealth, and happiness. Love and unity are ways to save humanity. Add this all together, and you will find the key to success and a planet in harmony and trust in God.

Author Bio

Antonia Gazetas Weese

Mother of one successful daughter, with four beautiful talented grandchildren. Wife of a great loyal husband, daughter of parents who were entrepreneurs, worked hard for everything they acquired. One sister who is a great educator, brilliant mind mother of two talented beautiful children. Antonia and her sister both entrepreneurs as well as their children handed down from their parents.

Antonia loves family, friends new and old, all creatures of the earth a believer of God and Jesus Christ and keeping the planet green saving mother earth.

Antonia is a healer, counselor, cosmetician, humanitarian, paralegal, writer, nutritionist, promoter and motivator. She loves life, people music of all kinds.She feels all God's children need to work and live together in peace. As a peacemaker Antonia has worked hard in life to be happy and help people to be happy. Her Grandchildren are her heart, they keep it beating.

Antoniagazetas@aol.com This book is written in hopes to help young adults to look ahead for life's punches, honor their parents, forgive all the wrongs and trespassers against them. Showing kindness instead of hate and anger will get you further in life. She has never liked bullies and feels bullies never have true friends or succeed in life. Antonia is in hopes of people using this book in the fine arts departments and reading literacy programs. this book is a means to educate people to live with all people in harmony and peace with all God's children.

Antonia Gazetas Weese strives to be a shining example of dedicated service, who will continue to promote unity, love, mentoring, teaching leadership and promote family activities to make a better community and nation.

Look for Antonia's new book coming soon, "Out of My Sisters Shadow" fiction based on true facts.This book is different it teaches you to be independent not co-dependent.

Last her holistic wellness cookbook will follow behind Called "Mother Goose Learns to Cook". People on diets, diabetics, high blood pressure, cholesterol and well being this cook book is for you.

Characters

Following is a list of the key characters, chosen from the Mother Goose stories.

Mother Goose: inspires and mentors children

Jack: won't do the right thing

Jill: a dreamer, but one who will strive to achieve her goal

Humpty Dumpty: made it; stopped taking dope and works

Clock and his Mice: are successful

Old Lady in the Shoe: has been successful in life

Little Miss Muffet and the Spiders: have lost their way currently; all are bullies

Yankee Doodle: wants to save the planet

Wendell the hairdresser: has a lot of compassion

Jeffrey the nail tech: wants to fall in love

Crusaders: planting trees to help Mother Earth and God's universe

Angel Singers

Dancers

Muffet's Posse: fellow students who are followers instead of leaders and miss good things life has to offer

Narrators

These are students of all ages and cultures, adults and youth all read together, tell the story. The music, as well as the actors; all together, you have a beautiful mix of people and a great educational experience.

You will find that there are directions for stage throughout the text that are set off in parentheses. The songs are numbered beginning with one and so on.

1. Intro "Mother Goose Theme Music" only small part

2. Song: "Doo Wah Ditty Ditty" just beginning part as Mother Goose walks out.
(Mother Goose comes on stage with lot of lights and colors. She gives thanks to God, welcomes everyone, and makes any credit announcements. The show begins; Mother Goose dances with dancers and singers to the song "Downtown.")

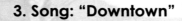

3. Song: "Downtown"

Narrator:
(Mother Goose Land set includes lights, music, dancers, and singers. Mother Goose finishes singing and goes right to her dressing room where Wendell, her hairdresser, is waiting for her to talk about doing her hair for the show. While discussing Mother Goose's hair, he brings her up to date on the characters from long ago.)

First Scene Set—Jill in her bedroom after graduating and receiving her GED.
(At stage left is a chair and table with a mirror and vanity. A cell phone sits on a table with a newspaper. Jill is sitting in her bedroom wearing her cap and gown from her graduation ceremony. She begins to sing of joy for her accomplishment as she sees the newspaper again and ponders the reality.)

Show Begins

Jill (Singing in the mirror as she dreams.)
4. Song: "Que Sera Sera"

9

Narrator:
Jill picks up paper after singing and finds interesting news.

Jill:
(As she thinks and speaks out loud, excited)
Mother Goose is in town. She is producing a musical Broadway production to help the youths of the community by expanding arts and integrating Reading, Math, Science, English, Communications, Mentoring, Leadership. All while students can earn credit for school in our area. The Broadway theater production cast members are optimistic of staging in New York. Gosh, a second chance to perform.

(Jill ponders.) Hmmm. Mother Goose is requesting her storybook characters, hoping they are still in town. Twenty years—wow, a long time has passed since we have all been together. I finally got my diploma. Staying focused gave me success in finishing my high school by attending classes at the adult education center and completing my GED. I can still go to college. Focusing on goals will give hope and faith that your goal will happen, just as long as you stay focused.

Mother Goose always said you have to follow your dream and go after what you want. She always did believe in angels. She said you are what you are because of who you are, bad or good. I guess who you are and what you achieve determines who you will become. Faithfulness and loyalty to anyone you work with will bring you far. Faith in God is all you need.

5. Song: "Follow that Dream" by Elvis Presley

Narrator:
The phone rings its Jill's best friend Donyella. Jill proceeds to tell her about Mother Goose being in town, but Jill's enthusiasm does not impress Donyella. However, is Donyella a good friend to Jill? People always say you should watch out for your friends.

Donyella is a young woman from

another land. In different parts of the world, people have a different way of life than they do in America. In the land where Donyella was born, life is different. She is in a one-way relationship. In addition, she has loved a man for a long time, but Donyella is not the only woman he loves. The only thing that Jill and Donyella have in common is that both women love men who have other women in their lives to love.

Nevertheless, the mothers of both women love and support their daughters, Jill and Donyella both have a bond that has developed between both women; one gives the other strength to carry on. Each gives the other advice on how the other should proceed in life. However, it is upon each of them to filter through their relationships and find their own way.

Donyella lives with her mother and son in a small but nice home. Jill is very close to her mother just like Donyella; both are in constant communication with their mothers. Sometimes Jill forgets that she is the daughter; her mom is her mom and not her friend. Parents, teach your children that friends are not always, as they seem and remember to be a parent, not your child's friend. In Jill's case, she will find that her newfound friend Donyella wants to be like her and wants what she has. One thing people should be aware of is do not want what someone else has. About the only thing Jill and Donyella have in common is that their mothers love them and take care of the children when their daughters are trying to find themselves. Grandparents go through a lot with their grandchildren, because the parents of the grandchildren just drop the ball, so to speak.

Donyella arrives at Jill's house after they briefly speak on the phone.

Narrator:
Remember, do not allow anyone to stop your dream. Focus on God's word and your life goals, and you will have guaranteed success.

Donyella:

Jill, I am sooo glad I caught you before you got on the telephone to call anyone. Tell me what is going on. Gosh, your kids are so lazy. At the age of five, I had chores where I come from. These step kids you are trying to be a mother to all of them will be over ten years old. They will not love you, as you think, this is the way they were taught. In addition, your man will not love your children as you would like that's how they think in my land maybe not all men but most including women. I know that my man does not love my son like his own. The little babies—they are so little, Jill. How are you ever going to try to be an actress/singer/dancer, run your business, and look after your kids? In my opinion, your man uses you. You are a doormat for him and his family. Wake up, girl, and see it for what it is.

Jill:

Well, Donyella, I started out early in life. Two children are from my first husband when I was very young. Three of those kids—Bunny, Knight, and Messy—are Neven's kids, who is my second husband. Now I am in my thirties, and I finally received my GED diploma, so my life will be different now I can go to college. In addition, the truth is that we do not even know if those three children are biologically his. Nevertheless, Neven is the only father they know; he is all they have. As for my oldest two—Playgirl and All-star—well, they have a deadbeat daddy, who is Jack, and he will not change. I believe their father has been seeing my aunt for years. Both my first husband and aunt are wrong for how they have acted through the years and treated me.

I still love both of my husbands—my ex-husband and my current husband Neven. I pray for both of them and I have forgiven both of them for the wrongs they have done to me. Faith, hope, and belief in God are all you need. Dreams and faith in God will pull you through any hard times in your life. As for my current husband, the two little babies God blessed me with Madame, who is two years old, and Prince, who is one year old; well, they are just fine.

As Mother Goose stated, follow your dreams. Listen, Donyella, close your eyes and listen dream a little. You have to make your dreams happen. You cannot

just sit around; remember that idleness is the workshop of the devil—remember that. We are all God's children, and I will love the children in my life who are not mine as if they were my own. I cannot help what has happened to them up until now. However, I can help them in their lives now, while I am in their lives. (**Jill Looks at the audience and speaks**.) You children out there, give your stepparents a chance to help you and love you.

6. Song: "Follow that Dream" by Elvis

Donyella:

Okay, Jill, later when the kids will get up—your two children and your three stepchildren—we will get this house in order and look after your husband's mother and the two little babies, Madame and Prince. Jill, seven children it is a lot. The training that has been given to your stepchildren—Bunny, Knight, and Messy—by their blood granny has not been good. If your three stepchildren were living with their father where his family was born, they would be paddled on their backsides for all the messes they make.

Children, when I finish talking to your stepmom, it will be time to come and see what is up with you girls. Your stepmom and I are good friends, and I will help her see the light. As for your daddy, and my man they do things that are not correct. Your granny knows all about it, but she acts stupid and she is not helping your father.

Jill:
Donyella, what is going on with the construction business? The man you love takes you away from what you should focus on. He is a man of many secrets and many women. I know I am taking care of children who are not mine. However, I made a commitment in this relationship to Neven I will try; I will treat those children as if they were my own. As for my current husband, Neven, I will pray for God to reveal the truth to me. Now listen to this tune try dreaming a little.

7. Song: "Follow that Dream"

Narrator:

As Jill ponders the future, she thinks about her life now. Jill is so young and has so many children. Jill has almost as many children as the Old Lady in the Shoe. One thing Jill does not figure is that when you have a friend, you should make sure that you do not put your whole heart into the relationship.

People in these days are not so sincere. Jill will find out that her dear friend Donyella is really betraying her with her boyfriend Villain. Jill has a clean heart that is about to be crushed. This is where family comes in to try to help her out of the horrible situation that is about to be revealed. Jill's husband Neven is unfaithful and betrayed his precious wife. The question here is will Jill survive all of this, especially when she finds out that the children who belong to her husband and the rest of his family are really using Jill for their needs. The Villain (Donyella's boyfriend), and Donyella, are both about to change Jill's world.

Friends need to be interviewed make sure they are God-fearing, or you should leave them alone. Jill wants to call Jack, her ex-husband and this is the perfect time to do it. However, before she does, she celebrates graduating and passing her GED test. She begins to sings a couple of old favorite songs that remind her of the past living with her first love and husband Jack.

(Jill stands in front of her bedroom mirror and sings partial tunes that remind her of Jack).

8. Song: "Here you come again" (As Jill sings, she dreams she is a model.)

9. Song: "Hard Candy Christmas" (Jill dances in angelic dreams.)

Narrator:
Look at Jill, she dreams of being a model, but she does not work very hard at her dream. Remember that in order to be a success in anything, you have to follow your dream, work at it, and be faithful in what you are doing. Have faith in God to bring you success along with your labor.

Practice all the time. It is your fault if a boyfriend, girlfriend, or anyone else stops you from doing and becoming what you want. Don't blame anyone, the blame is on you for being so weak, say no. Tell friends you can see them

later, after you are done with your work or practice. Follow your own rules if you do not, no one will listen to you, people and friends will walk all over you.

JILL:
(talking to herself and thinking about Jack)
Calling Jack is hard after I cut him out of my life. After all, he cut our children and me out of his life. He broke many hearts. Jack has never helped his family do anything. He always used my family, he had an affair with my aunt, and now he is having an affair with my cousin. I have to stop the hate that is in me and forgive Jack, my aunt, and my cousin. I must close the door on the great prince of darkness.

Wow, back then, I only had two kids (Playgirl and All-star), and they both belong to Jack. Now I have five more children, and three of them (Bunny, Night, and Messy) are my stepchildren. Neven's children, When I met him, he really did not know if they are truly his biological kids, but he claims them. He does pay the rent, but it is always late, and he buys food, but he gives no attention to me or the children, especially my two children from my first marriage. However, one day I will find the right man—a real man—and he will love all of my children as his own, My hopes he is not deceptive like the rest.

My stepfather used to babysit for my children. He loves them, and they call him Gramps. As for the mother of Neven's children, she abandoned her children. Life has a way of catching up with you.

Their paternal grandmother raised the children that I am taking care of but they were babies, six, seven, and eight years old, when I married Neven my second husband. His mother, she is an animal of a different color. From what I understand, this paternal grandmother and mother to Neven had nine kids by different daddies, and not one of those men loved her, as they should have. You cannot give love if you never received love. Granny became a taker and raised these children to be hateful, greedy, and jealous until I came along and rescued them.

Imagine—they simply do not know how to accept love, let alone give it. (**Jill looks at the audience**.) All of you out there, even if you are not loved, it is important to give love and live love so you can receive love. Remember that God's love is powerful and good. Due to my love for my second husband, his name is Neven. I did not give the attention to my own children, from my first husband Jack, and they suffered because of my wicked stepchildren and Neven they were all hateful to my first two children.

Nevertheless, this will all change. Sometimes I feel my life is gone, and I have no hope of true happiness. I should or I would—oh well, I have made it this far. God has made this path for me. In addition, I will surely give my best to follow it. People have to know it is harder than ever these days. Prices are going up on food, clothes, schooling, etc. Grandparents suffer a lot with the changing of insurance systems; they have raised insurance premiums and people have to drop their health insurance and be without health benefits.

Schools are no longer the way they once were. Teachers have rules put upon them; they cannot have any power over a student without a threat to the teacher. This makes it hard for both students and educators. Thank the Lord for our teachers who care and help us. I think I will call my teacher and see what she thinks. I am grateful she volunteered to be a mentor. People should know that even though you are a stranger to a youth, you could be a good adviser,mentor even save a life or a soul, and strengthen a family.

That is what I am going to do. Ms. G and Ms. T always helped and mentored me; maybe I will see if they will help tutor my children. Interaction will help my own biological children by being involved. I think I would like to become a teacher maybe that is what I will go to college for. I can be anything I want now that I have my GED its equivalent to my high school diploma. I was a little late finishing, but I have it. In addition, thanks to people like Ms. G and Ms. T, I will have the strength to reach that dream. I have been running my own construction business, and I have my difficulties, but I am a mover and a shaker. I can feed my own family, and that is a good thing. People out here in the community need to give peace a chance. Spread love, quit complaining, and speak positively Spend time alone for a while tend to the children no matter how many you have. God will lead.

10. Song: "Follow that Dream"

Jill: (thinking to herself)
Gosh! This is my moment!

Narrator:
Angels begin to sing about what Jack did to Jill in their own words.
(Lights go dim, and the rap tune is being performed.)

11. Rap Tune:
Jackity Jack and Jill went up the hill and started to have fun.
Messed around and fooled around, now they have a son.
She did not take the pill; he never wore protection. (What)

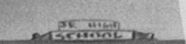

Can you believe they used no contraception?

They made a mistake, now they have to live with it. Raising a baby is no easy trip.
Jill settled down, but Jack did not bother.

Went on his merry way and again became a father.
Jack had two more kids, and he then settled down.
Not by choice, the HIV bomb dropped.
Jack is okay.
Lots of prayer, and he listened to the right kind of advice.
Therefore, the next time you want to poke around.
Remember sex is no joke, so do not fool around.

NARRATOR:
 Does Jill have the courage to call Jack and not worry what he thinks?
Can she call Mother Goose? Jill finds herself silent in prayer. Let us see what she will do next.

Donyella (walks in finds Jill silent in prayer and interrupts)
Jill, I feel you and your dream; you think I could make my dream come true?

JILL:
Yes, but first you have to believe in yourself. Your baby boy needs a strong father figure, the one you love is not his biological father, and he does not treat him as such you should allow the biological father to be in his son's life.

Nevertheless, your so called love, he still should be a parent figure, a good role model, and if he cannot, then he is selfish and out of order, and you must move on. You will find the right person to enrich your life. Money is not everything.

DONYELLA:

I know what you are saying. At times, it feels like family members, and sometimes other men and women, are only driven by money. It makes me sick to my stomach. They act like vultures feeding off whatever they can get.

Anyway, are you going to the Grecian Muse Day Spa to be prettied up before you go to see Mother Goose?

JILL:
Donyella, you only have one baby, I have seven kids to look after. I love them all just the same, but I just do not have money like that to go and get luxury things for myself.

However, good for you, Donyella, I am happy you can. I think I know the owner; we went to beauty school together while I was also getting my GED. She had it rough through the years, but she is a blessed woman with more children than I have. I wonder if she knows about Mother Goose.

DONYELLA:
Why is the Old Lady who lives in a shoe part of the group that Mother Goose is searching to find?

JILL:
We call her the Old Lady in the Shoe because her house is so small, like a tight-fitting shoe. She went to beauty school and graduated. She built her business by word of mouth and turned her beauty salon into a day spa.

Her entrepreneurial talents led her to build her spa by word of mouth, and she creatively made it look unique. I do not know about you, but I am just going to tell her the truth. Even though I do not have any money, she will still make me look good. We will have fun, Donyella, come and see.

To answer your question why Mother Goose is looking for the Old Lady in the Shoe, she was part of the original cast this is not Mother Goose's first show. Word has it that The Old Lady is having problems with her spa. She moved her spa to a resort where her husband and she were working. They invested a lot of their money, time, love, and energy.

I do not know, but they were taken by crime share not time-share. Word to the wise: watch out and make sure what you are buying is what you were promised and expected.

It is sad, but it feels as if we live in a deceptive world. The demon, as I call him,

who was in charge of that resort—I will not give his name—he made it very difficult for the Old Lady In the shoe. In fact, he lied to her. Moreover, in short, she lost her money, her vacation time-share, and her business all because a man who holds too much power was caught in his own web. Therefore, they had to cover it up and the Old Lady & her husband became victims The people also stole all her supplies real low down thieves in my opinion.

To make matters worse, her attorney let her down; he was on drugs and lost her case. The judge ordered him to rehab. That is what drugs will do—take you down.

However, remember that her faith in God and prayer brought her through. That is why she is in a place working most of the time free, because people just do not have money but others do, nevertheless she is making it. God bless us all.

DONYELLA:
You are so silly to worry about others so much, but of course, I will come. She is my hairdresser. I will tip her extra if she helps you.

JILL

You do not have to tip her on my account. I told you that she is as kind as she is qualified. I feel she will help me on my own accord. Look, Donyella, being a mom 24/7 does not mean you need to tip her extra for me. I stated to you that we know each other. Nevertheless, thanks for the offer. I will speak with The Old Lady myself.

(Donyella shows her jealousy by looking at Jill.)

Narrator:
Jill does not see what is going on in her friend's mind. Her friend is just plain jealous. As Jill stated, the world seems to be deceptive. As for her so-called close friend, she is jealous of Jill listen to what she is thinking Donyella is talking aloud.

DONYELLA:
(She is thinking aloud as jealous as she is.)
As I thought, Jill is so stupid that she sits at home and cannot even pay to get her hair done. Well good, so she knows people from her past who truly love

her—so she says.

I do not know what is going to happen when she finds out I am having an affair with the supervisor of her construction company. I need to be loved the right way, and I know my man does not love me. I will keep my baby's daddy and my current lover anyway, even if I am not happy. The money is what I am after, and as for the supervisor well we will just use each other for all the wrong reasons but I do not care.

I will make sure Jill's husband Neven is vaporized, meaning that I will get rid of him for a while. I will make sure he goes away for a very long time, as long as I can control the situation. I will make my man happy. Even though he is Neven's good friend and my lover, he wants Jill, so for the money, I will help him. In addition, as smart as Jill is in business, I cannot let her be successful, because then she will not need me.

I also have to try to get rid of her mother; they are too much like friends, the Mother Daughter relationship is what I would like to have with my Mother. Oh well, my man wants Jill, so I am going to sabotage Jill. I do care about her, but my man and money are more important to me. Therefore, I will go along with this until she finds out that I am trying to take her business, she will hate me.

The problem is that Jill so much believes in God that I feel guilty. In addition, there is the fact that she has always made me feel loved, and she has always cared for me. She should follow her own advice and watch what friends she really has. There is me, and then there is Jill's other friend, old Blondie. Jill thinks Blondie cares for her too. We do, but what Jill does not understand is that we are mad women, and even though she has many kids, they do love her, and she is loved by many. Even I love her. I just want what she has.

As for her other friend, Blondie, she is an addict. She does not know about motherhood. Really, I do not either. Our mothers have raised our children. Well, let me get going.

12. Song: "I'll Take You There" (Angel Choir sings)

Narrator:
Jill goes back home and calls her mother and grandmother. Let us watch. She is thinking aloud while in her room.

JILL:
(**Talking to herself**) I will call my mother and my grandmother. They will give

me inspiration. Grandmothers are so special; they have so much to give, and no one takes time for those precious Kodak moments that captures what life has to give us. That is why we should listen.

That is not going to happen to us. When you lose grandfathers and fathers at a very young age, you miss them in your life and all the advice that they give. Nevertheless, for me and my mother and grandmother, I will not miss those precious Kodak moments because I care and I talk with both my mother and grandmother.

Some of my friends have both mothers and fathers; they are so privileged. I still have a chance to see and talk to my father. My mother tells me that all the time. My mother and aunt always disagree; they just do not realize that life passes on, and it affects others. Anyway, it is my decision, and I will get in touch with Jack soon.

Narrator:
As Jill sits in her room, a thought comes to her mind. She looks at the paper as she sits on her bed she comes up with the idea that she is going to call Jack. First, she is going to get advice from her mother. Her mother knows how to find him, and maybe she even has his number.

Remember that Jill has no idea what Donyella is doing with her supervisor of the construction company and how Donyella is planning to take her business from her.

One thing, foolishly the supervisor does not see, is just as Donyella is betraying her best friend; she also is putting the knife in the supervisor's own back. Everyone will lose from this.

So now, Jill goes for her dream as betrayal is getting stronger, and Neven, the man from another land, she thinks he is loyal, yet he is plotting against her. Poor Jill, what is about to be revealed to her?

(Jill runs to the telephone, sits down, takes a breath, and begins to dial Jack's number) As Donyella looks at her, she sees a challenge coming. Jill has no idea how jealous Donyella is of her. Donyella works to look as good as Jill. Jill wakes up and still looks good; she has a natural beauty.

(The phone is heard being dialed, and Jill's mother answers.)

JILL'S MOTHER:
Hi, Honey, what is going on today?

JILL:
Oh, everything, Mom. Mother Goose is in town.

JILL'S MOTHER:
Jill, since the Day Spa business was brutally taken from us, just like the Old lady in the shoe, our partner, it has been so hard for us. That is what bad decisions and deception will get you, point is you have to research decisions you make and do not take a person's word. Jill your stepfather

really feels as if he has been kicked in the teeth He believed a man who ran things, had too much power and he lied to us just to get our money. Thank God, for your grandmother, your stepfather, and you, Jill, for the help you have given us.

After we heard about the Old Lady in the Shoe, we do not feel so bad. We are mad, but we are going to let it go. The only way to fight those giants who try to deceive people is by praying to God for them.

God is on my side, and we will leave vengeance to the Lord. God says I have to forgive so I will be forgiven. Remember, Jill, if Jack has not achieved anything, stay away from him. It is up to you; it is your choice. We have a different calling right now. We will find another way of making a living.

13. Song: "Smiling Faces"

Narrator:
You see, people, how important it is to watch all around you. It is so important to look closely at your friends, family, and strangers.

Make sure any business that you do is in writing. Listen and get advice from your parents or anybody else who might have experience in whatever it is you are going through. Look what is going on with Jill—she has no idea what is going on behind her back. She has to proceed blindly, because she trusts her friend.

JILL:
Mom, listen; please give me Jack's number.

JILL'S MOTHER:
Why? Jack is no good. I assume he is still lazy and not doing nothing with his life. However, if you insist, it is 865-437-6981. I do not even want to know what you are doing. The choices you make are important. Listen to your mind; do not go back and get involved with this man. I assume he has done nothing with himself. Not to mention that your new boyfriend wants to marry you. Is that still going to happen? I want you to know and remember deception! Your boyfriend loves you, but is he still married? Jack and his family all they do is use you. Jack's family is doing nothing with their lives. Jack has never helped you with the kids. Your kids were tossed aside, and you are allowing it to happen.

Jill, Neven, your soon to be ex-husband, is mentally abusing you and your

kids. Your boy is suffering; he has told me that when he gets a little older, he will beat Neven for abusing him. In addition, Donyella is no good. She sleeps around and is jealous of you; you need to watch out for her. I wish you could get away from all of those people.

Maybe it is true what my friend says about Neven's family. He keeps his mother there to make sure you are on lockdown. Think about it—he always blames you for stealing, while all along he gives money to others but not you, his wife. I am so happy that you finally are going to divorce him. Then you will be free to be with your new boyfriend who truly loves you, and you should marry him. Hopefully he is not a control freak, and he gets a divorce, remember your children are watching.

Remember that when someone does evil deeds to a person, it backfires and hits the one who is casting the curse.

Be careful Jill, I love you. Look at what is around you; you trust these people when all they know is to take from people and use them, these are bad people. I cannot understand how you got involved with them. Nevertheless, your grown, as you say, so the decision is yours.

JILL:
Thank you, Mom. If I can achieve it, Jack and I must at least be friends. We have kids together that Jack does know about, he just is trying to get away from paying child support, he will regret it. I love you, Mom, and I will try to bear it Thanks.

Narrator:
Jill's mom warns her of what she sees that is wrong, but some children just do not want to see the reality. As this story deepens, Jill's mind is on her dream to begin college she can start in fine arts maybe one of her dreams to be a star can come true now that she graduated from high school actually she passed her GED. She now can pursue her theatre life as she starts her career in the beauty business. This way she will be able to pay her way while in college.

Donyella sits and watches Jill as she calls Jack, and out of nowhere, Jill's mind is so loud that even Donyella can hear her thoughts. Jill has a love/hate relationship with Jack, but she has cleared her heart to forgive him. They do have children together, even though Jack does know about his children; he has no care for them. If he does not care for himself, he cannot love anybody. As always, parents grow old, children grow up, and they do not care about their parents because of how they were treated. Jill wants to tell Jack to

hit the road, but she has love for him and cannot tell him. We will see what happens next.

14. Song: "Hit the Road Jack"

(While the song is playing, Donyella exits, and Jill waits for Jack to answer the phone. She is anxious.

Jack answers the phone, and he is glad to hear from Jill.)

JACK:
Jill, is it you on the phone I am hearing? To what pleasure are you calling me?

JILL:
Yes, Jack, it is me Jill, How are you?

JACK:
I am fine. I think about you often. So tell me how in the world did you call me, and why? Before you answer that, are you married? Did you ever finish

school? I did not, but did finish my barbering school. I took the test but failed part of it, so I have not resumed it. I am not staying focused. Therefore, I never received my license. I bootleg, and I am still pursuing my music career. Okay, what is up?

Angels:
(Jack stops and remembers what the Angels are telling him. They sing the song to remind him.)

15. Song: "Hit the Road Jack"

Narrator:
Jack has always denied his son & daughter to get out of paying child support, as many do. Nevertheless, it is the children who suffer; they always have a void in their lives.

JILL:
Well, Jack, let me start by saying that I am happy that you finished school. No, Jack, I am not married, but I am engaged to be married. I came back to town to be with my mother. It is easier for me so that I can finish college. My beauty license helps me support myself. The reason I am calling you is to find out if you would like to come with me to visit Mother Goose. She is in town and wants to visit with her characters and find out what they are doing. She is doing a Broadway production, and I want to star in it what about you?

Narrator:
Jack will have guilt he has lost all those years of time he could have been a father to his two kids. Jill will be happy to see Jack; but will his kids be happy? Jack is a coward, he will not step up to the plate to help Jill with his kids. Jack is a deceptive person; what is his dark secret? Jill will have a lot reveled to her. This is what she prayed for; her faith will allow truth to be reveled too, this will set her free. However, as this story goes on, what Jill goes through is not going to be good. Just as the saying goes, the truth will set you free.

16. Song: "Respect Yourself"

JACK:
Look, Jill, I have my dreams, but I have to tell you that I did not do well in my education, so I have not been able to get my diploma. In addition, I have not succeeded in my music career. The only thing I have managed to do is getting back into beauty school, and that just happened. Thanks to the beauty school and day spa, I have worked everywhere. They help you with

jobs. They started a program called (Hire My Grandchild.) It has helped me make money. You know, I never did right by you. I would like to be friends again if you will consider it. Please call Mother Goose and find out if she will see us.

JILL:
are you going to contact Mother Goose in hopes she will give us a stage pass?

Narrator:
Again, Jill hurriedly rushes off the phone to see if they can be at Mother Goose's debut and be at her casting call. The love she has for Jack will always be there. After all of these years, Jill wants to help him.

JILL:
(She proceeds to get in touch with the theatre.)

Hello. Is this the theatre where Mother Goose is producing and casting for the production, I read in the paper. She wants to see her storybook characters and would like them to come and try out, Is that right?

Stagehand:
Yes.

JILL:
Great, I am glad I got the right number. Could you please connect me to Mother Goose?

Stagehand:
No, but you can make a trip down here. May I ask who is calling?

JILL:
Yes, of course, pardon my manners. I am Jill, and I will be in the company of Jack. Can you imagine, after all these years? I am excited and anxious. Whenever you have an open time, I will take it. An opportunity does not often come around a second time.

Stagehand:
Well, I am sure Mother Goose will be just as thrilled. She misses all of you, and she will look forward to meeting with you. Next week on Thursday at 2:00 p.m., will that work for both you and Jack?

JILL:
Yes, thank you see you Thursday Good-bye.

Stagehand:
 I am looking forward to seeing both of you on Thursday.

JILL:
Wow, I am glad that I am going to do something that is fun. Jack, on the other hand, who knows how he really feels. Again, as for the past, I have put it behind me. I am a forgiving soul after all, everyone deserves a second chance. Well, off I go, I will call Jack back.

Narrator:
Funny how life takes turns, as an old wives' tale I once was told says. Do not hold anger inside; give it to the Lord, and he will handle everything. It has been a long time since Jack and Jill have seen each other. Jack has always been a jealous soul and left Jill to proceed in his hobbies. As for his kids, he has done nothing and abandoned his children; shame on Jack. Parents, we will grow old, and our children will take over. I hope that we can have our children in our lives. In addition, children, look after your parents; they need you. The problem here is that Jack does not take care of his kids. The only thing that everyone does know is Jack has avoided working so he would not have to help with his precious children. All he accomplished is loss of precious Kodak moments, you can't put time in a bottle. He has other kids as well, and he does not take care of them.

Okay, Jill is now calling Jack.

JACK:
Hi, Jill , you got through to the backstage manager….

Thursday this week, Are you going? Sure, I will meet you at the stage door. It will be good to see you again Jill. See you soon.

Narrator:
Now what is going to happen? Whatever it is, Jill will have to deal with all of this, and again, her man (soon to be ex-husband) will betray her. Moreover, as for Donyella, who knows what will happen? First let us go back and see.

What is her so-called good friend Donyella going to do? Will she be that wicked to betray Jill. Why is it that you have a good friend, and your good friend takes your kindness for weakness?

Jill wants a friend so badly that she trusts these hood rats, so to speak. Just as Jill thinks her new friend is loyal, Jill thinks Blondie is her friend, as well as Donyella.

17. Song: "Smiling Faces"

Donyella:
Jill, I am having problems with payroll at our construction company. It seems that the supervisor never showed up on the construction job, so the client never paid us. In addition, the police stopped your husband Neven, and when they searched him, they found so much marijuana that he is in jail. You must leave school and forget about the theatre for now. Come home and fix this ordeal. You hear me Jill.

JILL:
Oh my gosh! I have to call my mother

Narrator:
Well, now it starts, poor Jill, what will she do? As Jill is crying, she dials her mother's phone number. Jill has not found out about the affair that her good friend Donyella had with the supervisor of their company. She does not realize yet that Donyella wants to ruin her.

JILL:
Mom, please just listen. Neven is in jail, and Donyella told me that the supervisor never showed up for the job. Mom, I will be ruined. Why is this happening? I am about to lose one hundred thousand dollars. I am so angry—so, so angry. What would anybody gain by this?

JILL'S Mother:
Jill, I will be over. I have some money and so does your aunt. We will help you get through this. Where is that Jezebel Donyella? You know that this is all her doing. As for Neven, well, just get him an attorney. I feel that the Villains are behind this.

Selling drugs and the greed of the money always catches up to you. I am so glad that now you will get rid of your so-called closest friend Donyella—how she ruined you, she probably is sleeping with the supervisor and trying to take your business away from you. I am not surprised about this. It is sad how some people have to control you or even sabotage someone else's dream.

My faith is strong, Jill. You have strong faith, and holding on to that is the only thing to do. Remember, Jill: dirty deeds done dirt-cheap.

18. Song: "Dirty Deeds Done Dirt Cheap"

JILL:
I was so hurt by Donyella. She just sleeps with anybody she comes across, and although I am not with Neven right now because he made bad choices and is in jail he is still part of my life, and I love him. I do not want this in my life or my children's life to be affected. Now whom can I call? Nobody but you Mom. I am so thankful that we are close. I hope that my aunt does not stress you. It seems that she is always putting you down and stressing you out.

Jealousy is a bad thing. Maybe one day you, Mother, and Auntie may get along. However, Auntie bashes everybody and has an excuse for her wrongs. All I can do is love her and let the Lord deal with it. I will get advice from you, Mother, auntie, and the angels, and I will pray. Everybody has to account for his or her deeds, good or bad.

Narrator:
See, parents are important to their children even if they do not show it. Children are very important to parents, so let us see how this evolves.

19. Song: "Dirty Deeds"

JILL:
Let me explain to you what has transpired, Mom. Mother Goose is here in town, she is putting on a Broadway production. I called and have an appointment with her on Thursday. I called Jack, and he said he would go. However, I found out that Donyella is having an affair with the supervisor, you were right, and they are trying to take my business away from me. They are going to my clients and telling them horrible things. Neven has gone to jail, and all I can do is bail him out and get him an attorney as you stated. Mother, call the police tell them how they stole my equipment and all the rest.

JILL'S Mother:
Jill, you are repeating yourself. I already know everything you are saying.

How much did Donyella and the supervisor steal? Anyway, go on with the meeting but remember to watch out for yourself and your feelings. Remember that it took a long time to get him out of your mind. Nevertheless, I have faith in you, so go on; just be careful. In addition, he owes his kids he should take

accountability for them. It is almost too late Allstar does not want anything to do with him Playgirl feels sorry for him. The children are getting older, and they remember.

Well, Jill, do what you want to do. As for the show, follow your dream. Call me later, get a good night's sleep, and tomorrow be confident with yourself. Okay, with that in mind, good luck. I love you, Jill. Get Jack out of your mind.

20. Song: "I'm Gonna Wash that Man Right Out of My Hair"

JILL:
I love you, Mom. Talk to you tomorrow. Good-bye.

She is so correct. I am over Jack, and frankly, I have the best part of him—I have his son & daughter. I will tell him that our son and daughter want no part of him. I am going to see the Old Lady in the shoe to see if she knows about Mother Goose. In addition, I want to be beautified before tomorrow. Let me get the number. Hello. Hi, Old Lady it is Jill, I am okay, and you?

Do you have time to see me? I need to see you, have my hair and face done, and get a mani/pedi. I really need you—your conversation is most important. You know, cosmetologists like you, Old Lady, are rare. I love the Day Spa.

Old Lady:

Sure, come over. We are getting busy, so hurry. Wendell will do your hair see you soon. What about your friend Donyella? You know, she was already here.

JILL:
Well good for her, I am on my way.

Narrator:
Jill is on the way to the Old Lady's Day Spa. Wendell is waiting to do her hair; he is one of the best. There is a party going on at the spa. This will be a lot of fun.

21. Song: "Your Hairdresser Can" (Sung to the music of "The Candy Man.")

Hey, Mr. Hair Mr. Hairdresser Man,
Hi everybody! Gather 'round. Your hairdresser's here!

31

What do you need today? Hair color—a marbleized, two-tone hair color. How about a facial, perm, relaxer? Maybe some hair extensions. Well, if you want to look good, come over here! Because your hairdresser is here!

Who can make your hair grow?
Sprinkle it with glue
Match up the color
With a miracle or two

Your hairdresser can
Your hairdresser can
Your hairdresser can 'cause he mixes it with love and makes the world look good.

Who can take a lotta hair?
Wrap it in a style
Comb it out, bump the ends, and make his client smile.

Your hairdresser can
Your hairdresser can
Your hairdresser can 'cause he mixes it with love and makes the world look good.

The hairdresser makes
All that he creates
Satisfying and expensive
Talkin' 'bout good times and wishes
He'll change your looks from rags to riches.

Your hairdresser can
Your hairdresser can
Your hairdresser can 'cause he mixes it with love and makes the world look good.

Who can take your new growth
Apply a little bleach
Bring it back to life; it's well within their reach

Your hairdresser can
Your hairdresser can
Your hairdresser can
'cause he mixes it with
love and makes the
world look good.

22. Song: "Great Balls of Hair" (words were changed to the original song "Great Balls of Fire.")

You did my nails and made me shout
You teased my hair, and you combed it out
You waxed my face
You wrapped my waist
Goodness, gracious, great balls of hair.
I laughed at your hair because it was funny
You changed your do, and you moved me, Honey
I changed your hair; gave it flare
Goodness, gracious, great balls of hair.

Perm me, Baby! Wooh it looks so good
Cut me, Baby
Girl, just let me style like a hairdresser should
Come over here
Sit in my chair
I'm gonna make my money doing hair, hair, hair, hair
I painted your nails and gave them zest
I'm real picky, but you're the best
Come on, Baby, hair is above the rest put me to the test
Goodness, gracious, great balls of hair.

OLD LADY:
Wow, I just love those songs. They really show how we hairdressers feel. Great tunes, you know, it will be very nice to see Jill, and I wonder if it is true that her so-called friend robbed her. I have told all my children to beware; you cannot trust many people these days.

The predators are out here in this world of deception. If the opportunity is there, people will take it. That is what happened to Jill; she lost everything to some Jezebel. Oh well, she will recover and grow stronger. What time is it? Jill will be here any moment.

Narrator:
Anyone can be their own boss if they stay focused and have faith in God and themselves.

Jill is about to walk into the Old Lady's business. Jill is sad but excited at the same time.

OLD LADY:

Welcome Jill, I have been so anxious to see you.

JILL:
Hi, Old Lady, Gosh, you look wonderful. Thank you for taking me at such a late notice. You have done well for yourself. In addition, you have all these kids.

OLD LADY:
First, sit down. You are so stressed, Thank you for your compliments. In addition, I will always take you in at any time. Understand, Jill that I care for you. It is not all the time that I can call someone my friend.

JILL:
Oh, I wish I could say that!

OLD LADY:
Well, I heard about that Jezebel. She tried to take your place. However, Jill, understand that she was never your friend. Be glad you woke up! However, look, you took that evil away. You will recover—first with a rejuvenation of your mind, body and soul. This is on me, you can make it up to me another time. Let's get you ready for Mother Goose. Now I will do your body and then your face. Wendell will do your hair, and at the end, we have Jeffrey, who will do your nails and feet. So now, we will get started. I will tell you some of my

34

stories, and you can forget your troubles.

Narrator:
As they get started, the Old Lady will sing a few tunes, starting with a song relating to her prior husband. The Old Lady and Jill will chat for a while. We will see what happens.

23. Song: "Frankie and Johnny" (Sung to the tune of the original "Frankie and Johnny; lyrics have been changed.)
Frankie and Johnny were hairdressers
Oh, Lordly, how they could do hair
They swore to be true, blue partners
And, all the money they would share
The idea was strong
They couldn't do no wrong.

Frankie was a bona fide artist
Johnny just wore the clothes
She started makin' lots of money
And Johnny put it all up his nose
It didn't take long
He was doing her wrong.

Now Johnny works along with a barber
Cutting hair for a buck or two
He said, "Frankie, you won't have the last laugh"
She said, "Johnny, Honey, the laugh's on you
My business is strong
'Cause you ain't doing me no wrong!

JILL:
Old Lady, that was a good tune.

Old Lady:
I'm gonna wash that man right out of your hair. I'm gonna wash your woes right out of your hair.

JILL:
Lady, you remember Jack. He is back; his kids do not want to see him. Not that I care, but tomorrow we go together to see Mother Goose. Well, I would like to just tell him to hit the road, ya know.

OLD LADY:
Yeah, I know. Jill, this is what I did to my man or any other man who mistreats me. It goes something like this.

24. Song: "I Am a Survivor" by Reba Macintyre
(Everyone sings and dances as Old lady continues to work on Jill.)

WENDELL:
Well now that you are all having fun bashing men, let me tell you all a thing or two.

Women can be very deceitful and very loving. Men and women do hateful things to each other, and that is a bad thing. After all those years, Mother Goose got married to somebody, somewhere, and they are very happy together. It is like the song from Reba. She sings, "Somewhere there's somebody."

Listen to this chorus. You have to leave yourself open so that you can meet someone. Quit being so negative against men, The kids hear all of this bashing, and then they start doing the same thing. Okay, Jill, sit down and enjoy. I am going to sing a song while I am doing your hair.

JILL:
Wait, Wendell, I have a song. Listen.

25. Song: "Somebody Somewhere" by Reba (Jill sings.)

Narrator:
After Jill sings, Wendell begins to sing, "If I Were a Rich Man" from the Broadway hit *Fiddler on the Roof*.

26. Song: "If I were a rich man"
JILL:
What happened to your wife, Wendell?

WENDELL:
She left me, divorced me. She likes, as she says, "her boys." She left me for other men who don't care for her. Nothing I do is ever enough—never, ever enough money. Really, it is all good. I really loved her, but it was not enough. So now, I am single. She has issues that extend back long before I appeared. I

am happy I met the Old Lady.

JILL:
Well, just as Doc Holiday said to Wyatt before he passed on, "Say goodbye to me Wyatt, and go on with your life. "Make one for yourself." It was something like that.

WENDELL:
Yes, you are right. It is hard.

Narrator:
Wendell is silent as he does Jill's hair, and the Angels above sing a song to cheer Wendell up.

27. Song by: Grass Roots (Lets live for today).

JILL:
Oh, Wendell, I love my hair. You are truly an artist. I know people appreciate you and your works of art. I will be meeting Jack at the stage door in about an hour.

Wendell:
Listen, when you are done, stop back by the park and join us for some pizza. We are all going to be singing and dancing. Some or all of the kids and some old cast members will be there.

JILL:
Okay, maybe I will, it sounds like fun, love you, Wendell, kiss Old Lady for me, See you later.

Narrator:
As Jill finishes up, the Old Lady is singing with her kids and some of the angels above.

28. Song: "He's got the Whole World in His Hands" (They are singing outside the courtyard. On her way out, Jill runs into all of them.

OLD LADY:
Come on, everybody, come, and sing, Jill, look behind you, It's Jack, Well,

what a coincidence, He's got
the whole world in his hands.
Narrator:
The group of people in the courtyard continues singing. As the song is almost over, Jack takes Jill and they begin to go to the theatre stage door. It looks like they're adventuring
down the path. Let us
watch, as they are to meet
with Mother Goose.

29. Song: "Alley Cat"
(Jack and Jill dance their
way to the stage door as
old friends. They are looking
forward to meeting Mother
Goose.

Stage door officer:
How wonderful to see the
both of you. Mother Goose
is looking forward to seeing
all of you. Come in; go
down the corridor, turn left,
and follow the signs to the
parlor. Mother Goose is having private spa services.

JACK:
Thanks.

JILL:

Yeah, thanks, Guard. God bless you.

Narrator:
Jack and Jill are trotting down the corridor in an adventure to see Mother Goose. They can hear Mother Goose and others rehearsing.

30. Song: Put a Little Love in Your Heart"
31. Song: "New York, New York"
32. (Repeat) Song: "Alley Cat"
(The alley cat shuffle is performed by Jack and Jill)
Narrator:

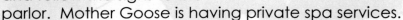

Jack and Jill finally arrive to the parlor where Mother Goose is awaiting them. As they look at each other, Jack wants to know what Jill has done all these years. In addition, Mother Goose begins to catch up with the two and tells them all about the rest of the cast.

Before their arrival, Mother Goose has time to talk with Jeff, her nail tech and dear friend. She is also waiting for Wendell, her hairdresser, to come from the salon to do her hair back stage.

Mother Goose:
Jeff, it has been a long time since I have seen you. In addition, I know you still do not have your life in order. However, come work with me, not for me. You

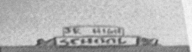

should have your own nail business by now, so let me help you get on your feet.

Jeff:
Thank you, Mother Goose. I know you are right. What is going on with you?

Mother Goose:
A lot, Putting this show on helps me forget my problems. Giving to others spreads a little love and entertaining keeps the arts alive and helps some of the kids and parents. I want to bring families together and help them become stronger. Wendell is here waiting, so we need to finish up. Plus, here come Jack and Jill. Jeff, take care of yourself. I want see what Jack and Jill are doing.

Jeff:
Yeah, well just as you say, I will pray for myself. I just wonder, Jack was so cruel to his wife and did nothing with his kids. However, I will be supportive do not worry.

Mother Goose:
Well, well, here you are finally. You both look so good; come in. Jill, I see that you have been to see Old Lady and Wendell. They did a good job. Jack, you could have gone as well. How is the barbering business? Well, anyway, come and let me catch you both up on your friends. Then I want to hear about both of you and what you have both done.

Mother Goose:
I have heard that Little Miss Muffet has been last seen at school and is said to be very incorrigible. There are some wicked spiders after her that she seems to think she can play with. The Clock is doing very well with his mice. The Old Lady in the shoe, well, you saw her and her associate Wendell. She has all of those kids, and she still works and goes to school. She is almost ready to receive her degree, and do not forget that she is an entrepreneur. Humpty Dumpty was all cracked up from that horrible drug, but I do believe that with help from his good friends, family, and school, he has finally been put together again. Where are you two going?

JACK:
In answer to your earlier question, Mother Goose, yes, I do well at barbering. I still have to get my license. We are headed down the road to see everyone in the neighborhood known as Mother Goose Land. The city was named after you, Mother Goose.

We want to see who is around sing and dance until it is time to perform and get our scripts. Maybe we can help find everyone.

Mother Goose:
Okay, Jack, both of you go on. I have to rehearse before opening night. Love you both.

33. Song: "New York, New York"

Narrator:
As Jack and Jill proceed, they go carefully. They do not know what they will run into. First stop, the Clock, What will Jack and Jill see and hear from him, and how do Jack and Jill feel about one another?

(Lights go dim on the path they go down.)

34. Song: "Alley Cat"
(Jack and Jill dance to the song and arrive at the Clock's house. The Clock and the mice are dancing to the song that is being sung.)

35. Song: "Life Is but a Dream"

(Lights are down on set. Only floodlights are on behind the singers, which are angels singing with them.)

JACK:
Wow, look, Jill. The Clock is really looking good for his age, and it looks like he is well off.

JILL:
Jack, it is as Mother Goose said. He was doing well with his business of fourteen years. He had to work hard to achieve his goal. He did not let anyone come in his way; and, he

finished school. Anyway, let us go in and talk awhile. I am so impressed.

JACK:
Yeah, okay, I want to know his secret of success.
Moreover, I want to know how he has had his partner for so long.

Narrator:
Jack and Jill look on as the Clock is working. He is singing, and he and his help are all so happy. Jack looks as if he has lost out. Well, let us see what they are about to hear from the clock.

After the song, the Clock looks over and sees both Jack and Jill.

CLOCK:
Oh, my gosh! How the heck are you two doing?
You both look good. It is nice to see you both together as friends. I know you are not a couple anymore.

JACK:
Okay, okay. Yeah, we just reacquainted today. Jill called me to say that Mother Goose is back and that she is going to do a show. In addition, I guess you, like all of us, are here at Mother Goose Land to perform. We do not have to even cast, because we are, in fact, the stars.

CLOCK:

Okay, Jack. Yes, you people are the stars, but so am I, along with my partners. Mousey and her sidekicks we do well as a team. Mother Goose is allowing me to be in the show we already casted. We are getting ready to rehearse the song. Would you like to join us as we rehearse just for fun?

JACK:
Hey, if Jill is up for it, why not. Sure, I would like to be part of it.

JILL:
Of course. It would be fun. What is it?

CLOCK:
Well what do you think? One, two, three and hit it.

36. Song: "Rock Around the Clock"

42

(The music starts, and all begin to jitterbug to the song "Rock Around the Clock.")

Narrator:
All are having a good time. After the song is over, the Clock and Jack talk about their dreams and how he achieved it. Jack and Jill proceed down the road and dance right to a picnic that Old Lady is having with all of her kids and Wendell, who has a crush on her. When Jack and Jill arrive, they begin to eat and sing.

37. Song: "Amore"
(Characters on stage sing along with the audience.)

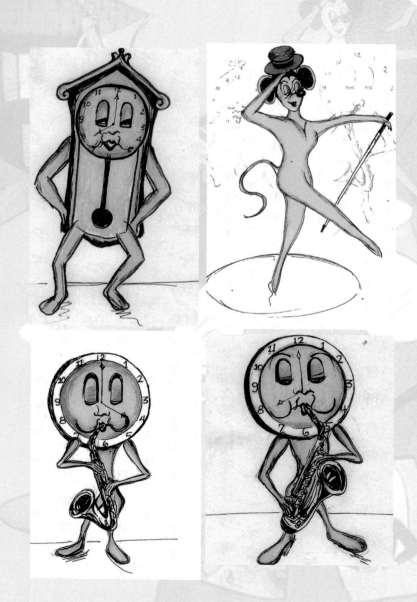

Narrator:
Mother Goose arrives, and all join in and sing "Amore." Mother Goose talks to friends and warns them about what they should be cautious of.

Mother Goose:
Kids, the world has become a jungle out there. Times are so bad these days. There is a song—actually, two songs—that rather describes the way I see the world. Start the music, Jack, and let's sing and dance.

38. Song: "It's a Family Affair"

39. Song: "Ball of Confusion"

Narrator:
Mother Goose plays these songs to make a statement to everyone. This is the world through Mother Goose's eyes. They all sing, and angels are singing with them. The children join in and begin to sing.

40. Song: "On the Good Ship Lollipop"

41. Song: "This Is the Way We Wash Our Hands"
(A young girl, who appears to be Muffet, sings.)

42. Song: "Shoop Shoop song it's in His Kiss?"
(Jill watches Muffet sing and then joins her. After the song, Jill answers, "Yes, it is.")

Wendell:
Go, girls, all of you sing and please give some of that inspiration to all of us. Please, sing again.

Before you sing again, listen to my "ABC Rap" song.

43. Song: "ABC Rap"

Please listen,

Attitude, gratitude
Bountiful brains
Courage to face the
Downs when it rains.

Etiquette, etiquette
Funky but cool
Great to live the Golden
Rule
Hold back your temper
Idle your tongue
Joking and jesting is lots of fun
Kick up your heels and
Let down your hair
Make with the merry; see how
It feels
Now
Open your mind
Put yourself in command
Que up your talents and
Rig up a plan
Set your sights high
Think everything through
Use all your wits to make
Them come true
Verily, verily
Words without end
X
Y
Z means zing it again

How's that for a quickie?

44. Song: "He's got the Whole World in His Hands"

WENDELL:
Hey, come over here. It is useless at this time to try to talk to Muffet. She is too head strong and will not listen. The best thing to do is let her go.

Look, it is Jack and Jill.

(Jill joins the kids singing)
(Muffet sings)

45. Song: "Coat of many Colors"

(Jack and Jill leave the party and find Humpty Dumpty.)

JACK:
Hi, Humpty Dumpty, you are looking good. We know you were in trouble awhile back, but it looks like you came through it.

Humpty Dumpty:
Yeah, I was hooked on crack. Some of my friends did crystal meth, which is just as bad. Then you need a pill to call yourself mellowing out. Listen, I do hold a job, and I pay all my bills. Ha, I have lots of money—no drugs, lots of money. If you have done drugs, you understand what I mean. The same is true of having an eating disorder or smoking cigarettes—all of it is like a drug addiction, even shopaholics. They are all addictions.

I was telling Wendell not to beg Muffet anymore. People have tried, especially her auntie has tried to talk to muffet, and Auntie has been through tough times in her life, her sister has abused her. Muffet's mother has let her go do whatever she wants to. Now her auntie has repositioned herself. She is trying to pay all her bills and repent and spread the word. In addition, she is working to forgive all and live with love. Listen to a rap I wrote. Then I will sing a song.

46. Song: Rap tune is sung by "Humpty Dumpty

Back in the day there was a boy named Humpty Dumpty.
Who started smoking dope and drinking brass monkey.
Everything was fine and dandy at first.
Money was going out to quench his thirst.
Burst like a bomb, problems started to erupt.
Little Humpty Dumpty found himself in a handful of dump.

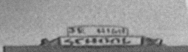

He jumped on the gun had to pay off his debts
Two years in prison was how his life was spent.
When he finally got out, he got back on the pipe.
A toke over here, a toke over there; running around wondering where that next hit of that poison would come around
Strung out like a junkie doing that bomb.
Knowing it's wrong, he was on the street going through garbage to find something to eat.
Went from penthouse to a sewer in matter of time.
All from smoking that rock and snorting those lines.
It's over
He did become sober
Because he knew hell was not ready to freeze over.
He stopped.
Humpty Dumpty did too much and almost OD'd.

47. Song: "Black and White" by Three-Dog Night

48. Song: "Everything Is Beautiful"

Wendell:
Okay, Humpty, I understand. I will go back to my old lady. She is beautiful.
God bless Muffett.

Humpty Dumpty:
Yeah, Wendell, you better. I have eyes on her. You keep playing the streets at night, something might happen.

JACK

Bye, Wendell, see you later. Humpty, that rap was great and so was the song. That was an old tune, but old is good. You have been blessed for coming out of all those dark days and helping others the way you do. Give and you will receive.

Humpty Dumpty:

Thanks, I try to make wise choices and live humbly, but it is hard. I do not run after money. Sometimes a little is good. I believe in Jesus; he is my friend and savior, and if you believe in him, you will have it all. I even wrote poem called "World of Crack." I pray all the time.
Listen to the poem.

As I kneel here in front of God
I want him to hear my plea for help
Dear God,
I'm entrapped in the world of crack
Satan has a hold on me and that's a fact.
Only you God can set me free and bring me back to the life I once had

Satan my Lord is coming on strong
My faith in you oh Lord will not allow myself to fall, Storm clouds are gathering.
God, I know you will hold my hand and stop the tremble

I know I'm doing wrong
As I ask you Lord, to forgive me and save my soul only God knows how low I can go

Satan is coming he will not go back the drug that Satan has cast will take us down really really fast
Remember my friend you can help too
Work with God; have faith in him too
Then you will have the power to send Satan back down to the land he has found.

God is our friend, and if I die, I have faith that God will send Satan away Only God can save our souls
So all of you out there on crack listen well.

Stop the drugs because Satan will tell then he will come and take you to hell.

48

Humpty Dumpty:
So how did you like that poem?

JACK:
(Jack and Jill look at each other. Jack tells Humpty how good it is that he is changed.)

That was great. We want to see you again. Look, let us catch Muffet before she splits.

Little Miss Muffet:
Well, I would like to sing some more, but my posse is awaiting me at school.

JILL:
How are you doing in school these days?

Little Miss Muffet:
School is boring to me. I am tired of being bullied all the time from kids that have no lives. Their parents just do not have the time to spend on them. Sometimes they do; other times, they do not. Take my mother, for example, she is a screamer. She does nothing but complains and blames her mother or sister, but she is the real loser. She is losing time. But then, so am I; I follow in her footsteps. I just really do not give a care, so there you have it. I am miserable—like my mother. I'm almost out of school but money and drama at home has caused me to flunk a year.

JACK:

Ah, Miss Muffet, it sounds to me like you are assuming your mother's role, but the reality is you really do not have an excuse, I guess it is your mother. Plus, Muffet, you have gained weight, and you use this as an excuse just like me I have turned my back on responsibility and also my drinking as you're eating let's face it the obesity is what is making you lose your voice and making you irritable. In addition, you are not a nice person as you are. Muffet, just take the plunge. Look at me; I am almost forty. You are half my age.

Do you think that all the screaming your mother does is out of love and to wake you up? Here is what I sing.

JACK:
49. SONG: "KING OF THE ROAD"

JILL:
This is what I sing
50. Song: QUEEN OF THE HOUSE

JILL:
We do not want you to end up in our shoes Muffet; you are still young
Education is the answer it's your ticket to ride wherever you want to go in life

Narrator:

Jack has never come forth to take responsibility for his two kids. This is where reality sets in; Muffet tells him he is a deadbeat dad Jill begins to sing.

51. SONG: "ANGEL BABY"
Her love for her kids is her priority. She lives for her kids they come first now; she used to put men that she thought loved her first.

MUFFET:
Look, Jack, you do not know anything. What are you still doing? Writing songs—ha—using women to get you by. What about your kids? I heard you have several. You do not take care of any of your kids; you are selfish. Jill has been used by her men, she thinks the latest one is her knight in shining armor. Well, I am sorry, Jill, I think that as smart as you are, you are just plain stupid.

Actually, why are you both here? I am skipping school, and my friends and I are going to hang out. Teachers cannot teach me anything, and I don't care to learn, so what's the point? Teachers are mad that they are not paid enough. They, too, are tired of the bullies at school. The parents of the bullies are sometimes bullies themselves. There is no ending to this; at least, I do not see one. Bullies are losers, so they jump on others to make themselves feel like big shots.

Now, other than that, excuse my friends and me. We are about to leave. Oh yeah, layoffs—lots of that going on. I wonder if we will have enough teachers to go around. We kids have to watch out for predators. Everywhere you go you find some sick person, some creep who cannot live a normal life. I mean, what's up with that?

You have to be careful of being abducted, molested, or seduced. My life is a confused mess. I do not even work! Why? Depression. My mother is always fighting with my aunt. My mother has been through it with us kids. We have disrespected her so much. Life goes on, and now we are getting older. My sister is wrecking her life. She is not doing well right now. She has been mentally abused and at the same time has been spoiled. So now, she is in danger of predators coming after her because she feels she knows the streets. The problem is that the predators can live in your own backyard. My teacher said it could be anyone, even a distant relative, or a friend. My aunt says that these people will have to answer to God. I have a problem with all of this.

Narrator:
While all this is going on Spiders have noticed that Muffet has weakened they begin to sing.

52. SONG: "MY GIRL"

JILL:
Well, Muffet, yeah, I am stupid but not that stupid. I have come out of my shell, and I have faith in myself. All you say is the truth, I have heard that your mother is quite rough and a control freak, but then you are of age now. You cannot blame her for leaving. You were blessed with a voice. Your choice in men is bad; don't do what your mother has done. Do for yourself school is so important, regardless of the bullies. Just like you said, their parents are bullies, and they are mad. They feel good when they can control people, but you are a leader, so lead by giving a correct example, not by skipping school. The teachers need help, not to be ridiculed. Where are you going right now?

In addition, you have finally met a good man. He works. Is that not half the battle?

Muffet:
Yeah, Jill, but I do not love him like that anymore. He works all the time, but so what? He has not accomplished anything—just like Jack.

JILL:
Well, Muffet, you stated that you are confused. Go to work; get something to do. Have you realized that your problems are all solvable? No man will stay with you if you treat people poorly, and you will find yourself nowhere. You best pull it together.

Jack:
Leave her alone, Jill. Can't you see that she is not responding? Let me sing a song that might put some light on the matter.

53. SONG: "EVERYDAY PEOPLE"

JILL:
Shut up, Jack! You are a little lost too. Ante up to what Muffet is saying—you do not take care of your children, however many you have. You are a deadbeat daddy. Face it—you are a bum. Muffet is right; children can only learn from what they see and hear.

Many rock groups only play foul music. They have lyrics about using girls as toys and doing drugs. What do they have to follow? Parents these days barley have an education, so they hold two jobs to make ends meet. They carry two jobs on and on and on.

Muffet, I can only say that there is always hope. In addition, no matter what your parents have done, you have to live for yourself and live for today. However, most of all, you have to forgive and move on.

54. Song: "Live for Today"

Narrator:
Jack and Jill watch as they listen to the song that Muffett sings along with her posse. While Jack and Jill are listening, they are amazed at the talent these kids have. They find themselves thinking about how they wasted so much of their lives to others. It is like the words that John Lennon and Jim Morrison wrote before they died tragically. John Lennon was brutally taken away from us,

and Jim Morrison overdosed on drugs.

(Angel singers sing)
55. Song: "PEOPLE ARE STRANGE" by JIM MORRISON

56. SONG: "IMAGINE" by John Lennon

MUFFET:
You know, people, it would be nice for the entire world to be as one. It has been so hard for me. My mother and I have been through so much, with our family feuds, which have been so violent. We kids have been lost in the shuffle. Nobody seems to listen—all the adults have lost their way, and we kids had better get it together. I feel so lost sometimes, but God brings me through. One thing I have learned from this experience is to be independent and not depend on people. If home is bad, stay in school. Like I said, I am almost done with school.

In addition, do not wait to get your education. An education is the ticket; it's important to earn a degree or learn a trade. Nevertheless, learn something. I forgive everything anybody has done to me, and I leave the past in the past. It gets you nowhere. Live for today and focus on tomorrow.

In addition, have faith in the Lord, and you will be okay. Money is not the answer. Love one another; we do not have to carry the hate that our parents want to carry; it is not our battle. The world is a ball of confusion. People do not like people, and that is not how God planned it.

School is very challenging for many young adults besides me. The heartaches I have had in school and at home have depressed me. In addition, living with a brilliant mother who was teaching in the school system is not easy, I always have to be making high grades and set the example.

Narrator:
Jack and Jill look in sadness as they watch Muffet walk off into the streets.

57. SONG: "SUNRISE, SUNSET"

Narrator:
As the plot thickens, the spiders are very aware of Muffet being weak, and now the spiders are bragging on who is going to get Muffet after they abduct her.

SPIDERS:

58. Song: "MUFFETT RAP"

Little Miss Muffet sat on her tuffet eating her curds and whey. Along came a spider and sat down beside her, and guess what he started to say?
Excuse me, little girly, your looking kind of lonely.
You want a lollipop or ride on my pony?
She replied yes, and they were on their way.
Poor Little Miss Muffet may not see another day.

They were all searching, looking around. No one knew that Little Miss Muffet was hidden about eight feet underground.
How could this happen? The spiders seemed so nice.
Little Miss Muffett was saved, so she did get to see another day.

Little Miss Muffett who was hidden eight feet underground.
Just remember: when you come across a stranger, you always think twice.
The next time a person appears to be nice, it's usually fake.
So do yourself a favor and do not make the same mistake.
She couldn't say no.
Ignore strangers; nowadays, saying no is the only way to go.

MUFFET:
My auntie always stated that not all strangers are bad. Don't profile interview new acquaintances and check ID. Point is do not make an assumption make sure who you are talking to.
I will be eighteen just like the song.

59. SONG: "Eighteen"

Spiders:

We have answers for you Muffet, Spiders sing their answers to her.

60. SONG: "You Can't Always Get What You Want"

Narrator:
Do not forget, everyone, that Jill wanted Muffet to understand what she said.

Women, don't depend on men, and men, don't depend on women. Nevertheless, if you have an education, then you will have a job. You can depend on yourself. Nowadays it takes two people putting their money together to survive. Women and men who think that they do not have to work just become slugs. They loaf in bed or just become so lazy that they lose a lot in life.

Spiders:
Where are you going? You have money?

MUFFET:
Well, I do not need money like that. Anyway, we are skipping school, and I am going to hang out with my friends.

Spider:

61. SONG: "GET A JOB"
Muffet, you had better watch out for those friends. Look out for yourself in those streets where you are hanging with your friends.

Being around strangers and dwelling in the streets can be very dangerous. You may be abducted!

MUFFET:
I ain't got anything to fear. I am sure not taking orders from you guys, I was telling a person named Jack, what a bad role model he is. You spiders are all bullies,

and you have not lived properly that is why you spiders all live in the streets. Moreover, you have a house but you do not fix it you have a big hole in your roof.

Listen to this song, maybe this will help you understand me.

62. SONG: "YOU DON'T OWN ME" by L. GORE

Narrator:
Jack and Jill look perplexed and concerned Watching Muffet going down the street. Thinks she has it going on. Muffet's man is stepping out on her, and she thinks life is good. What is this young girl thinking? Muffet is going down a street she does not know anything about. Remember that people, places, or things might look beautiful, but all that glitters is not gold. Listen, young people, watch out. You may not respect anyone, but respect yourself. Do not forget that people are strange.

63. Song: "People Are Strange"

Narrator:
All the spiders were watching Muffet leaving the school grounds. They are talking amongst themselves, pondering when they should leap. They want to grab Muffet. They begin to sing a song as they choose which girl of her posse they will take to be theirs.

64. Song: "Big Girls Don't Cry" by The Four Seasons

65. Song: "I Feel Good" by James Brown

Narrator:
The spiders are mad and angered that Muffet has all the opportunity and is just throwing it out the door. The spiders feel that they have lost out in life due to their parents and the fact that they grew up poor.

(Spiders sing.)

66. Song: "Sixteen Tons"

Narrator:
As the spiders planned and abducted Muffet, they are prepared to show her how they feel and live through songs. Could the spiders and Muffet see the

light of their failure, rise above it, and come together? Let's watch and listen while they all sing about their lives so to speak.

67. Song: "Don't Let the Rain Come Down"

Narrator:
Listen, everybody, the spiders are on a hate note. The spiders are angry they do not want to forgive anyone. Listen, everyone, I will play a couple of songs for you. Maybe we can all work together and change the world.

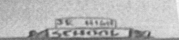

68. Song: "What the World Needs Now is Love"

69. Song: "Put a Little Love in Your Heart"

SPIDERS:
Look, Muffet you think you can come down our street. We got you; let us show your spoiled self what the street is all about. We have been casted out of society because of our mistakes and our evil ways.

BIG DADDY SPIDER:
Hey there, girly, where you going?

SPIDERS:
Yeah, where you going? Ha ha.

MUFFET:
I am skipping school, and I got lost. I cannot find my friends.

Big Daddy Spider:
Do not worry, we will help you

MUFFET:
Really? That would be great. Thanks.

BIG DADDY SPIDER:
So what happened to make you skip school? Your parents or your teacher? Alternatively, both? Do you work? How old are you?

MUFFET:
Gosh, what is with all of the questions I am eighteen, and yeah, the teachers are off the chain meaning they want more money, which they deserve. They have to understand that as students, we don't know what to say because students don't know how to help the situation to make it better for the teachers, this makes tension thick in schools today...

You feel me. My mom has always been with me but my Dad I do not know

him.
He's been out of our lives since I was seven months old. My mom has had a tough time she is a teacher and a single mom. I don't want to be around her while she is miserable. My point is I am fed up with adults putting their problems on our backs it is not fair.

SPIDERS:
Come on leave her alone, Big Daddy. Let us sing a tune; we are performers sit and listen missy we are good at heart we just made some mistakes.

Narrator:
Miss Muffet trusts the spiders. They used their music to lure Muffet into the dark forest where they live in means to abduct her and Muffet does not see it coming, that is why you must interview who you talk to.

People come in all forms, sizes, and shapes. Do not forget that they can be good or evil. How you protect yourself from evil is to put all your trust into the Lord and take him as your personal savior. If you do that, it is guaranteed that you will have his blessing. Listen to warnings; do not be so rebellious. Even if you are mad, let someone know where you are going. Give the phone number of the person you are with to someone else for security.

Spiders:
We will show you what you really have and now where you really are. We are not your friends. We are evil—you know, demons—and we are going to make your life miserable. You people allow us in your lives through music, movies, and books. We demons want you to work for us. We want the oppressed and those like you.

Muffet:
Well, all of you might be evil, but there is one thing you do not know—I am capable of being on the side of the Lord. You all have not done your homework. I believe in Christ the Lord, and he is my personal savior. So do what you feel like. You might as well let me go, because people will look for me. My mother or my cousin and aunt will all look for me. You Spiders sing songs that can make you feel better, or they can make you sad and mad. Different artists' tunes make the world go round. The music world has contributed to society's children. The selection is up to you.

America stands for freedom, unity, and the pursuit of happiness. Other people and we Americans should get along, and the world would be a better place. All I know is that as Americans, we are free. You all have no reason to abduct me. Remember, we are one nation under God, indivisible, with liberty and justice for all. I have not broken the law, so just because you all are mad, you want to take it out on me. You evil spiders, go back to your dark and dismal place, because I will never comply. Keep your ways to yourself. Listen, I have a song for you.

(Angel singers and Muffet together sing.)

70. Song: "There's No Love Left in the World"

Narrator:
Well, at this point, Muffet has a problem. Now she has to try to get out of a situation; meanwhile, everyone is looking for her.

Word has gotten to Yankee Doodle of her capture. Let us see what happens next. She knows now for sure that there are demons—many of them. They are in human form. However, do not forget the angels. They fight the demons all of the time. We need to help them. Do not give in to the devil and his demons. Let us watch and listen. Mother Goose has told people that Muffet is missing.

Yankee Doodle:
(He is checking whose missing and talking to himself.)
What is this Amber Alert about? Muffet has been abducted! Gosh, that girl really does not listen to anybody. I need to help with the search. People really need to be alert, because not only are abductions a big problem, but

terrorism is just as bad. Anymore in America, we the people must get a grip on abductions, terrorism, pedophiles, predators, deadbeat dads, and even deadbeat moms.

People use kids (some even use their own) for money. Some may even use children as advantage to keep parents in a hole or maintain control of a spouse or ex-spouse. All of this has to stop. It has become part of our schools. One thing people can do is share the responsibility of any children they have together. They should not be afraid that they will be sued or hide their wages. People can help the world. We could stop suicide among our youth and adults. We must forgive all people; most people do not know what they are doing when they make bad choices.

71. Song: "Yankee Doodle"

Narrator:
What do you think about these spiders? Yankee Doodle is really a hero going after Muffet, and he goes around warning people and their children about strangers. As long as we believe in one God and freedom, nobody will be able to hurt you, and that will be hard to top. Yankee Doodle loves life and the earth. Our ancestors created our independence for us. Yankee Doodle has tried to stop the overdevelopment of land and encourages people to replace the trees by planting more trees, plants, and vegetables. However, he is now taken away from this quest to help save Muffet.

YANKEE DOODLE:
Here I am, wondering how I will find this lost young youth before something happens to her. These young adults, male or female, it does not matter these days. Some people are out for kicks and getting high. These days they do not give us adults much hope for us to feel confident in them taking over where we leave off. Anyway, gather 'round, people, and let us sing a song. What is this, Jack and Jill? What are they doing? Let me go see. Hey, you two, Jack, Jill, what is up?

Jack
Hey, Yankee Doodle, what a surprise. We were so worried about Muffet; actually, we were just about to sing a few songs to dedicate to Muffet.

72. Song: "No No Song" Ringo Starr

73. Song: "Kicks" Paul Revere and the Raiders

61

Narrator:
Everyone is sad over Muffet being missing.

MUFFET:
Well, spiders, what are you to do with me? Please let me go. This must have my mother-worried sick.

Spiders:
Hmmm. We do not know what we will do at this time. We want to play with you. You feel us. You are the one who put yourself in this position.

Muffet:
I never thought I would be so frightened. However, if you harm me, you will not get away with it. People are looking for me right now; I know this. I feel like singing.

(As Muffet begins to sing the song, the spiders sing with her.)
74. Song: "I'm Not a Juvenile Delinquent"

Narrator:
Muffet holds her head up and sings. She sees that the spiders really are not so bad. They really want to come back to society. She knows that she has a chance, so she prays to herself.

75. Song: "The Greatest Love of All"

Narrator:
As Yankee Doodle finds out where the spiders hide out is, he prepares a posse and goes after Muffet.

Spiders:
Hey, man, let us sing a song for Muffet. Hey, Muffet, sit down and listen to us.

Narrator:
Spiders are afraid that they will go to jail for abducting Little Miss Muffet, so they are trying to get on her good side. Muffet is also scared and has convinced the big spiders to release her. Let us listen to what the spiders are trying to tell her.

76. Song: "Backstabbers"

Spiders:
You know, Muffet, it's only minutes before we are caught. We have a song we all want to sing to all the mothers. In addition, Muffet, forgive us. Maybe we can be friends. In addition, look out for each other. We all have to live together as one. That is God's will.

77. Song: "You Are Appreciated"

Muffet:
Yeah, well, I am crying. I made a big mistake. I am so mad that when something good happens, I do not even know it. The world is crying. I have lost sight of our morals, and when I escape, I will help fight you demons. In addition, if I die in your hands, then I will be an angel of God. I will work for him, and I will give myself to God. He will help me.

Narrator:
Muffet has zoned the spiders out; she does not realize that they want to be friends. They want to get her home and maybe start their lives over. That can happen no matter what age you are. Boy, Muffet has herself in a mess. She may not be set free. However, God will prevail and maybe even the spiders will be set free, and they can have a second chance.

Narrator:
Look, this is driving those demons away. Everybody knows that good will always prevail over evil. She still loves and believes in God.

Spiders:
Oh, gosh. Muffet, can you help us?

Muffet:
(She looks and feels sorry for the spiders.) You will not break me. I will pray to God, and I will prevail in escaping you spiders.

Narrator:
Muffet does not realize that the spiders are about to let her go.

Spiders:
Look! What is Yankee Doodle doing coming into this neighborhood? What do you think? To rescue Muffet? Well, let us take her farther down. No, let her go. If anything, we, for once, can do something good. We are always doing bad things; we had better do a good thing. What? You feeling guilty?

No!
However, we do not want to get in trouble. All we do is bully people.

MUFFETT:
Yeah.

SPIDERS:
What are you talking about? Muffet, you hold first place in being a bully, and so is your mom and sister. Tell the truth—are you not tired of bulling everyone? That is why you are always miserable, because you are not happy. You have to be in control all the time. Anyway, your prayers are answered. We are going to turn you lose. Now go, run, and let Yankee Doodle find you.

MUFFET:
Thank you all. Hey, Yankee Doodle, here I am! The Lord heard me. He answered my prayers. I owe him, and now I will help others. The first thing I will do is give my part to help. Ten percent of whatever I make when I work I will give to the poor or church—that is the rule. In addition, help those in need like other kids who do not understand what is happening. Our world needs love.

78. Song: "I Only Want to Be with You"

YANKEE DOODLE:
Thank you, Lord, for bringing her back to us. I feel like singing. We do love America; we should all stop the wars.

(Yankee Doodle and his posy all sing.)
   79. Song: "War"

JILL:
Look, Jack, Yankee Doodle saved Muffet.

Jack:

Yes, I know, Jill. Will you give me a chance to try to make things right with my kids? In addition, thank you for not putting me in jail. I just wish you had communicated with me sooner.

JILL:
Jack, that is no excuse, but yes, I will give you another chance. We can be friends. Besides, no one knew where you were.

Muffet:
Well, everybody, the lesson has been learned. Think before you act or make choices. Watch out for strangers. Be kind and do not be a bully. No one likes bullies—not even your own family. Do not steal or lie and stay in school. Your diploma is your ticket in any goal you will want to achieve. Love one another. Honor your mother and father. Love makes the world go round.

(Mother Goose, Jack & Jill, Yankee Doodle, Wendell, Humpty
Dumpty Little Miss Muffet, Clock, Old Lady, and the rest of the cast all sing
together)

80. Song: "Everything Is Beautiful"

81. Song: "What about Us" by Mikael Jackson

82. Song: "God Bless America"

CURTAIN